TENDER HOOKS

TENDER HOOKS

POEMS

BETH ANN FENNELLY

W. W. NORTON & COMPANY

NEW YORK LONDON

For information about permission to reproduce selections from this book, write to
Permissions, W. W. Norton & Company, Inc., 500 Fifth Avenue, New York, NY 10110

Manufacturing by Courier Westford
Book design by Chris Welch
Production manager: Anna Oler

Library of Congress Cataloging-in-Publication Data
Fennelly, Beth Ann, date.
Tender hooks : poems / Beth Ann Fennelly.— 1st ed.
p. cm.
ISBN 0-393-05862-X
1. Motherhood—Poetry. 2. Mother and child—Fiction. I. Title.
PS3556.E489 T46 2004
811'.54—dc22

2003026072

W. W. Norton & Company, Inc., 500 Fifth Avenue, New York, N.Y. 10110
www.wwnorton.com

W. W. Norton & Company Ltd., Castle House, 75/76 Wells Street, London W1T 3QT

1 2 3 4 5 6 7 8 9 0

*for Tommy
and for Claire*

CONTENTS

I

Bite Me   15

Three Months After Giving Birth,
  the Body Loses Certain Hormones   19

Latching On, Falling Off   22

Interpreting the Foreign Queen   30

Gong   31

Extra   32

Favors   33

"If Only We Could Keep Them Small Forever"   34

Once I Did Kiss Her Wetly on the Mouth   35

II

Waiting for the Heart to Moderate   39

Night Game   41

Land Where My Father Died   42

When I Tire of Houses and the People in Houses   44

We Are the Renters   45

I Need to Be More French. Or Japanese.   47

A Study of Writing Habits   49

Why We Shouldn't Write Love Poems, or If We Must,
    Why We Shouldn't Publish Them   54

III

On Collaboration: Downward Dog,
    Happy Baby, Cobra   59

Telling the Gospel Truth   65

Riddle, Two Years Later   84

The Gods Watch Us Through the Window   86

Making an Egg for Claire, Sunny-Side Up   87

The Presentation   88

IV

Having Words with Claire   103

Say Cheese   109

Driving the Spoon into Her Mouth   110

First Day at Daycare   111

Lo, the Child Displayeth Cunning,
    Paradise Is Fayling   112

Daddy Phase   114

The Gods Tell Me, *You Will Forget All This*   117

ACKNOWLEDGMENTS

"Driving the Spoon into Her Mouth," "First Day
at Daycare," and "Gong," *Blink*
"*Daddy Phase*," "Lo, the Child Displayeth Cunning,
Paradise is Fayling," "Making an Egg for Claire,
Sunny-Side Up," and "Waiting for the Heart to Moderate,"
The Cincinnati Review
"On Collaboration: Downward Dog, Happy Baby, Cobra,"
The Connecticut Review
"Latching On, Falling Off," *The Crab Orchard Review*
"Bite Me," *The Georgia Review*
"A Study of Writing Habits," *Gulf Stream*
"Night Game" and "Three Months After Giving Birth,
the Body Loses Certain Hormones," *The Harvard Review*
"Telling the Gospel Truth," *The Kenyon Review*
"Extra" and "The Gods Tell Me, *You Will Forget All This*,"
Meridian

"The Presentation," *The Notre Dame Review*

"'If Only We Could Keep Them Small Forever,'"
   Poetry Miscellany

"I Need to Be More French. Or Japanese," *Ploughshares*

"Once I Did Kiss Her Wetly on the Mouth," "Riddle, Two
   Years Later," and "Why We Shouldn't Write Love Poems, or
   If We Must, Why We Shouldn't Publish Them," *TriQuarterly*

"Land Where My Father Died," "We Are the Renters," and
   "When I Tire of Houses and People in Houses," *Wind*

"Bite Me," "I Need to Be More French. Or Japanese," "Once
   I Did Kiss Her Wetly on the Mouth," "We Are the
   Renters," and "Why We Shouldn't Write Love Poems, or If
   We Must, Why We Shouldn't Publish Them" appeared in
   They Write Among Us (Jefferson Press).

The author wishes to thank her family, especially her mother.
Thanks also go to Carol Houck Smith for the dogwoods and
raindrops, Ann Fisher-Wirth for the sparks, David Baker for the
road map, and most of all, Tom Franklin, still and always *more
than friends*. In addition, the author wishes to thank Knox
College for its humane policy of parental leave, during which
many of these poems were begun, and the University of
Mississippi's Kathryn Black Summer Research Fellowship, during
which many of these poems were finished. Generous financial
support from the State of Illinois Arts Council and the National
Endowment for the Arts made this book possible.

The world was so recent that many things lacked names, and in order to indicate them it was necessary to point

—GABRIEL GARCÍA MÁRQUEZ,
One Hundred Years of Solitude

I

BITE ME

You who are all clichés of babysoft
crawl to my rocking chair,
pull up on my knees,
lift your delicate finger to the silver balloon
from your first birthday,
open your warm red mouth
and let float your word, your fourth
in this world, *Bawoooooon—*
then, delighted, bite my thigh.
I practice my stern *No.* You smile,
then bite my shin. *No,* I say again,
which feels like telling the wind *No*
when it blows. But how to stop you?
This month you've left your mark on me
through sweatshirts and through jeans,
six-teeth-brooches that take a week to fade
from my collarbone, hip, wrist.
What fierceness in that tiny
snapping jaw, your after-grin.
You don't bite your teething rings,
don't bite your toys, your crib,
other children, or your father.
It makes us wonder.

Daughter, when you were nearly here,
when you were crowning
and your father could see your black hair
and lifted in his trembling hands
the scissors to cut your tie to me,
when a nurse had gone to the waiting room
to assure my mother *Just a few more pushes,*
when another had the heat lamp
warming the bassinet beside my cot,
then held up the mirror
so I could see you sliding out—
you started turning. Wriggling
your elbows up. The mandala
of your black hair turning and turning
like a pinwheel, like laundry in the eye
of the washer, like the eye of the storm
that was just beginning
and would finish me off, forever,
because you did it,
you got stuck, quite stuck,
and so, they said, I'd have to push
head–shoulders–elbows out at once.

And Lord did I push, for three more hours
I pushed, I pushed so hard I shat,
pushed so hard blood vessels burst
in my neck and in my chest, pushed so hard
my asshole turned inside-out like a rosebud,
pushed so hard that for weeks to come
the whites of my eyes were red with blood,
my face a boxer's, swollen and bruised,
though I wasn't thinking then
about the weeks to come
or anything at all besides pushing and dying,
and your father was terror and blood splatter
like he too was being born
and he was, we were,
and finally I burst at the seams
and you were out,
Look, Ha, you didn't kill me after all,
Monster I have you,
and you are mine now, mine,

and it is no great wonder
that you bite me—

because you were crowning
and had to eat your way out of me,
because you were crowning
and developed a taste
for my royal blood.

THREE MONTHS AFTER GIVING BIRTH, THE BODY LOSES CERTAIN HORMONES

And my hair starts falling out.
Long, red hair on the sheets, clogging
every drain, woven through the forest
of my brush, baked into brownies,
every shirt a hair shirt, hair inexplicably
in the spider's web, my husband's books,
cinching my daughter's wrist—

this shedding stops in a month, I read—just another
Thing They Never Told You About Childbirth,
like how I've gotten my first cavity,
like how sneezing squeezes out a drop of pee—

at least they told me to expect this body,
how it's soft and soupy now, my flesh
hanging loose from my bones,
this, while the child's skull is hardening,
her fontanelle fusing its portal
beneath her cap of magnificent hair.

Yes, she is growing up and I am dying down.
If I can hope for, say, another thirty years of dying
that old consolation can console.

Another thirty years seems far away,
and I'm feeling elegiac, comfortably elegiac,
watering these impatiens hanging from the porch,
baby on my hip. It's foolish, perhaps false,
to view my life with this grandiloquence
but even the suddenly slowly dying need indulgences:

Child, I've loved many things, I've loved food heartily,
I've doubled the garlic in every recipe,
I've had the perfect peach and understood,
I've taken a night train and woken
in a new country, owning little,
I've hitchhiked and the man who stopped
sang me opera all the way home,
I've loved jokes, the ocean, anything with sequins,
the Mississippi juke joint and the man there
with a hook for a hand
who spun me gently on the dance floor.
That I've loved my work occurs to me now,
I've been fond of almost every student,
and the one time, moved by a poem,
I wept in class the way I'd always feared I would
the students did not laugh at me, at all.

I have loved most your father, my partner
in dying, though perhaps he doesn't know he's dying yet—

My hair knows
my hair, surfing westward on the breeze,
is saying goodbye to this world
to its bows and braids, its sequins and stroking fingers,
my hair, anticipating everything—

Who else knows?
The house finch,
building, in the basket of impatiens, her nest.
The eggs in her body are hardening, ripening,
ready for her to start dying—
the house finch, busily weaving
with strands of long, red hair.

LATCHING ON, FALLING OFF

I. When She Takes My Body into Her Body

She comes to me squirming in her father's arms,
gumming her fingers, her blanket, or rooting
on his neck, thrashing her mouth from side to side
to raise a nipple among his beard hairs. My shirt sprouts
two dark eyes; for three weeks she's been outside me,
and I cry milk to hear my baby—any baby—cry.

In the night, she smells me. From her bassinet
she wakes with a squall, her mouth impossibly huge,
her tongue aquiver with anger the baby book says
she doesn't have, aquiver like the clapper of a bell.
Her passion I wasn't prepared for, her need
naked as a sturgeon with a rippling, red gill.

Who named this *letdown*, this tingling upswing?
A valve twists, the thin opalescence spurts past the gate,
then comes the hindcream to make my baby creamyfat.
I fumble with one hand at my bra, offer the target
of my darkened nipple, with the other hand steady
her too-heavy head. She clamps on, the wailing ceases.

No one ever mentioned she's out for blood. I wince
as she tugs milk from ducts all the way to my armpits.
It hurts like when an angry sister plaits your hair.
It hurts like that, and like that you desire it.
Soon, soon—I am listening—she swallows,
and a layer of pain kicks free like a blanket.

Tethered, my womb spasms, then, lower, something shivers.
Pleasure piggybacks the pain, though it, too,
isn't mentioned, not to the child, drunk and splayed
like a hobo, not to the sleeping husband, innocent beside us.
Let me get it right so I remember: Once, I bared my chest
and found an animal. Once, I was delicious.

II. First Night Away from Claire

I forget to pack my breast pump,
a novelty not in any shop
here at the beach, just snorkel tubes,
shark teeth, coconut-shell bikini tops.

Should we drive back? I'm near-drunk
from my first beer in months. We've got
a babysitter, a hotel room, and on the horizon
a meteor shower promised. We've planned
slow sex, sky watch, long sleep.
His hand feels good low on my back,
tracing my lizard tattoo. And he can help—
he's had quick sips before—so we stay,
rubbing tongues, butter-dripping shrimp.

Later, he tries gamely, but it's not sexy,
not at all—he needs to suck a glassful
from each breast. The baby's so much better.
He rests. *It's hot,* he says, *and sweet.*
We're tired. We fall asleep.
I wake predawn from pain.

Those meteors we forgot to watch—
it will be thirty years
before they pass this way again.

III. After Weaning, My Breasts Resume Their Lives as Glamour Girls

Initially hesitant, yes,
but once called into duty,
they never looked back.

Models-turned-spokeswomen,
they never dreamed they'd have so much to say.
They swelled with purpose,

mastered that underwater tongue,
translating the baby's long-vowel cries
and oozing their answer,

tidal, undeniable, fulfilled.
For a year, they let the child draw forth
that starry river, as my friend Ann has termed it—

then, it was time, stopped the flow.
They are dry now, smaller, tidy, my nipples
the lighter, more fetching pink.

The bras ugly as Ace bandages,
thick-strapped, trap-doored,
too busy for beauty—

and the cotton pads lining them
until damp, then yeasting in the hamper—
all have been washed and stored away.

So I'm thinking of how,
when World War II had ended,
the factory-working wives

were fired, sent home
to care for returning soldiers,
when my husband enters the bedroom—

Aren't you glad? he asks, glad,
watching me unwrap bras
tissue-thin and decorative

from the tissue of my old life,
watching, worshipfully, the breasts resettle
as I fasten his red favorite—

Aren't you glad? He's walking
toward them, addressing them, it seems—
but, Darling, they can't answer,

poured back into their old mold,
muffled beneath these lovely laces,
relearning how it feels, seen and not heard.

IV. *It Was a Strange Country*

where I lived with my daughter while I fed her
from my body. It was a small country, an island for two,
and there were things we couldn't bring with us,
like her father. He watched from the far shore,
well meaning, useless. Sometimes I asked
for a glass of water, so he had something to give.

The weather there was overcast, volatile.
We were tied to the tides of whimper and milk,
the flotsam of spit-up, warm and clotted,
on my neck, my thigh. Strange: I rarely minded,
I liked the yogurt smell trapped beneath her chinfolds.
How soon her breath bloomed sweet again.

She napped, my ducts refilled
like veins of gold that throb though lodged in rock.
When she woke, we adjusted our body language.
How many hours did she kiss one breast or the other?
I told her things. She tugged my bottom lip,
like sounds were coins beneath my fascinating tongue.

We didn't get many tourists, much news—
behind the closed curtains, rocking in the chair,
the world was a rumor all summer. All autumn.
All winter, in which she sickened, sucked for comfort,
a cord of snot between her nose, my breast.
Her small pillows of breath. We slept there, single-bodied.

Then came spring and her milk teeth and her bones
longer in my lap, her feet dangling, and, rapt,
she watched me eat, scholar of sandwiches and water.
Well, I knew the signs. I held her tight, I waded out,
I swam us away from that country, swam us back
to my husband pacing the shore, yelling and waving,

in his man fists, baby spoons that flashed, cupping suns.
It was a strange country that we returned to, separately—
strange, but not for long. Soon, the milk stops
simmering and the child forgets the mother's taste,
so the motherland recedes on the horizon,
a kindness—we return to it only at death.

INTERPRETING THE FOREIGN QUEEN

I rush home after class to slurp her thigh,
to pounce on baby belly, press my lips deep
to spray wet-raspberry kisses. They make her writhe.
I'm spilling giggles, nibbling ticklish feet.
My husband, the anti-tickler, disapproves.
He says she'd just been resting in his lap,
she'd just had food (she's always just had food)—
now, overstimulated, she won't nap.
He swears I shouldn't toss her, not so high.
She gives a shriek—pure terror, pure delight?
We read our own emotions in her eyes.
If only she could speak to say who's right—
to say *I* am. For him, I put her down.
Just two more days till he goes out of town.

GONG

From the kitchen, fixing her bottle, I hear it:
two milk teeth against my beer can.

EXTRA

It's happening:
my daughter's
heavier. I hold her
& she grows
down. She'll hit
the ground running.

An old movie,
& in the background
an ancient woman
carries against her chest
a sack of groceries.
It gets away
from her. All
that pretty fruit
rolling in the dirty street
& how bereft
her arms look, hugging air.

FAVORS

People look at my baby and wonder whom she favors. Because she doesn't look like me, they decide she looks like her father. I nod. I nod and nod. But really she favors the great dead one. My own bad Dad. She favors him, the same brown eyes, the same scooped out philtrum, that valley leading from nose to mouth, as if the warm fingers that formed her stroked a perfect pinkie tip there to sculpt it, a valley filled with orchards where dusk brings cinnamon-velvet deer who crunch sweet apples beneath the bee-buzzing, white-blooming trees. See, I love her, so even from the grave he spites me. Look at him, winning again, crying in the bassinet. Here I come on quick feet unbuttoning my blouse.

"IF ONLY WE COULD KEEP THEM SMALL FOREVER"

—Slogan for infantwear

Your knees are polished apples, all week
you've scoured them across the shag,
practicing your commando elbow-heave,
and then, on Sunday, officially, Your First Crawl.

Your knees, those scrubbed potatoes, are ringed,
as if I'd tried to eat you, wearing my red lipstick,
starting with those most scrumptious knobs.
And, of course, I have, swooping you up

like a pelican to pack you into my mouth,
pressing you against my stomach, that suitcase
gaping at its former freight—how did
it fit? It's hard work for you to crawl

to the sharp-cornered, glass-topped table,
and hard work for me to let you. *That's enough, now.*
Shhh. Your heart, the size of a plum, thumps
against my thumbpads. In my lap, you wriggle,

reach for my dinner plate heaped with beef.
Never again will you be so tender.
By your age, calves are slaughtered,
because, milk-fed, they have the best flavor.

ONCE I DID KISS HER WETLY
ON THE MOUTH

Once I did kiss her wetly on the mouth
and her lips loosened, her tongue rising like a fish
to swim in my waters
because she learns the world
by tasting it, by taking it inside.

I desired it—her learning my tongue that way.

Yes, I wanted to soul-kiss my daughter,
to lather, slaver the toothless gums
and the cat-arched back of her palate,
to sniff the bouquet of baby's breath
all the way to the vase of her throat

Look at her, in her highchair,
wearing her yam goatee

I like to take her whole foot in my mouth

Look at her, in her bib
slung backward, like a superhero's cape—
beware, small villains everywhere

Oh, that first day
when the nurses returned her to my cot
so newly minted, her soles were black from ink
they laid her, naked, on my naked chest
so she could swell my breasts with milksong,
so I could warm her skin with my skin,
and so, next to my more regular heart,
her skittish beat would steady—
though I swear when she latched on
all meter, music changed

I whispered in her see-through ear
I'd keep her safe forever—
I, her first lover.

II

WAITING FOR THE HEART TO MODERATE

Adults had a drink, they said, *to take the edge off,* so that's how she came to understand growing up: erosion. She was all edges, on *tender hooks*, which is what she thought the expression was. Once she described this to her mother, and her mother assured her it would pass. It kept not passing. In a few years, she'd lie to her mother, drive to the city, and wait in line beside the dance club, hugging herself beneath her growing breasts. What would this studious girl do, once she got inside? Climb the risers and dance in a cage. For her, it was not about alcohol or Ecstasy, at least not the kind you bought. In that strobe-light dark, the music saw the music she had coming from inside and raised her twenty decibels. She danced for hours, quelled her frenzy a little. When she left, her ears felt cotton-muffled, the Chicago streets hazy and desolate like a movie without enough extras, her sweaty clothes stiffening in the freezing wind.

She is twice as old as she was then, but here she is, thinking that everything is yet to come. She is still the chimney with its fire going, and the sparrow trapped in the chimney. It's hardest in the caffeinated spring when her corneas are azalea-scorched, when the neighbor girls stroll to the Howorths' pool, unself-conscious, and flick the rims of their bathing suits that have crept a bit up their backsides. Watching from the window, the mirror, she knows she isn't one of them, though she still likes best the clothes in the *junior* section. Even having the baby hasn't moderated her as it might have. The sitter comes over, and they are wearing the same outfit. She knows her social-worker sister would call this *inappropriate*. She is by no means that slim young girl anymore, but how hard it is not to say, late into the party, *Let's toss our clothes aside, hop the Howorths' fence, and go nightswimming! Let's pile in some cars and race to the Gulf!*

Let's see. After the years of fevered dancing came the years of fevered travel (and all along, the fevered years of men), then the years of trying to settle in the town with the train that each morning would set the dogs to howling and set her edgy heart to howling alongside them. Now she lives in a town without a train, but it doesn't help. What helped: yesterday, she held her teething baby across her chest, and the child first gummed her collarbone and then bit, really bit, so hard the woman yelped. Six red crescents from the child's six teeth. For a moment, nailed to the here and now. And she loves the here and now! So why does she still want to dance all night? Why does she still feel music booming in her breastbone? Do others guess that something wild paces in this cage? She fears that, to free it, she might do something stupid.

NIGHT GAME

The parents of my generation are dying,
the last line of defense.

We're floodlit now, pals,
we're casting shadows,

the shapes of our bodies
distinct on this earth.

Who will catch
the pass,

the ball that's sewn
from skin?

LAND WHERE MY FATHER DIED

Improbable Illinois—so flat
you'd see a whole train, engine to caboose,
crossing the prairie at a distance—
seems a lifetime away.
But it was not so long ago
I kept a newspaper on a passenger seat
for when the freight train beat me to the crossing—
ten minutes of my life gone, twelve.

Mississippi's better.
A simple proclamation.
I'm at the age when I trust
the simple. Here on my porch,
it's cold beer and cricket-racket,
and lovely Audrey, envoy from that old land.
Who, apropos of the light show
in the darkening yard, says
lightning bugs are disappearing in Illinois.
Hadn't I heard it on the radio?
No, but I can guess the story,
the hybrids and insecticides, the tiresome
lessons we keep not learning.

The night is long, and wide.
In the land where my father died
the last ones awake
shuffle through quiet houses
snapping off the lights.

WHEN I TIRE OF HOUSES
AND THE PEOPLE IN HOUSES

I think of the highway from Alma to Fayetteville,
how it shaves through fresh and forested hills,
hills without houses anywhere.

In my mind I build the sole house upon that hill.
In other cars, other drivers build there, too.
So the land is ruined by our dreaming.

Surely there are other vistas, roadless, unbeholden,
with hills that ripple, with ground as tensile as the skin
of a wild horse that feels the smallest fly. Yes, just like that.

No, not like that. Land like that
would resist even metaphor. Land like that
would not comfort us. Land like that would not conspire.

WE ARE THE RENTERS

You need no other name for us than that.
The good folk of Old Taylor Road
know who you mean. We are
the renters, hoarders of bloated boxes,
foam peanuts. When the Welcome Wagon
of local dogs visits our garbage,
we're not sure which houses to yell at. So
what if we leave the cans there a bit too long.
We have white walls, a beige futon, orange
U-Haul on retainer, checks with low numbers.
Scheming to get our security deposit back, nail holes
are spackled with toothpaste. Ooops, our modifiers
dangle. Our uncoiled hoses dangle, but the weeds
in our gutters do not, they grow tall,
they are Renters' Weeds, they are unafraid.
An old black one-speed leans against the carport. So
what. Maybe we were thinking about riding
past these houses with posters for Republican governors.
We have posters, too: *Garage Sale.* "Can I hel—"
"No, just looking." We are just looked at, we renters.
Are we coming soon to *your* neighborhood?
We're the ones without green thumbs,
with too many references, the ones

whose invitation to the block party
must have gotten lost in the mail. If we're still here
come winter, tell the postman not to bother
searching our nameless mailbox for his Christmas check.

I NEED TO BE MORE FRENCH.
OR JAPANESE.

Then I wouldn't prefer the California wine,
its big sugar, big fruit rolling down my tongue,
a cornucopia spilled across a tacky tablecloth.
I'd prefer the French, its smoke and rot.
Said Cézanne: *Le monde—c'est terrible!*
Which means, *The world—it bites the big weenie.*
People sound smarter in French.
The Japanese prefer the crescent moon to the full,
prefer the rose before it blooms.
Oh, I have been to the temples of Kyoto,
I have stood on the Pont Neuf, and my eyes,
they drank it in, but my taste buds
shuffled along in the beer line at Wrigley Field.
It was the day they gave out foam fingers.
I hereby pledge to wear more gray, less yellow
of the beaks of baby mockingbirds,
that huge yellow yawping open on wobbly necks,
trusting something yummy will be dropped inside,
soon. I hereby pledge to be reserved.
When the French designer learned
I didn't like her mock-ups for my book cover,
she sniffed, *They're not for everyone. They're*
subtle. What area code is 662 anyway? I said,
Mississippi, sweetheart. Bet you couldn't find it

with a map. OK: I didn't really. But so what
if I'm subtle as May in Mississippi, my nose
in the wine bowl of this magnolia bloom, so what
if I'm mellow as the punch-drunk bee.
If I were Japanese I'd write a tone poem
about magnolias in March, each bud long as a pencil,
sheathed in celedon suede, jutting from a cluster
of glossy leaves. I'd end the poem before anything
bloomed, end with rain swelling the buds
and the sheaths bursting, then falling to the grass
like a fairy's cast-off slippers, like candy wrappers,
like spent firecrackers. Yes, my poem
would end there, spent firecrackers.
If I were French, I'd capture post-peak, in July,
the petals floppy, creased brown with age,
the stamens naked, stripped of yellow filaments.
The bees lazy now, bungling the ballet, thinking
for the first time about October. If I were French,
I'd prefer this, end with the red-tipped filaments
scattered on the scorched brown grass,
and my poem would incite the sophisticated,
the French and the Japanese readers—
because the filaments look like matchsticks,
and it's matchsticks, we all know, that start the fire.

A STUDY OF WRITING HABITS

1. Found Poem: Rejection from Richard Howard

Is there nothing slimmer?
Nothing shorter, sleeker,
tighter, less self–
consciously poetic, in other
words?

2. It's a Doggy-Dog World

for poets who grow up to be comp teachers
because our spelling is recked forever
so are our idioms and old wise tales

a student writes of the novel
that won "the Bullet Surprise"
it drives her "out of my mine"

It's good to keep a sense of humor
if your name sounds like "beta amphetamine"
and you find yourself thinking
when you're supposed to be sleeping
a bullet surprise would be fine

*3. On Marianne Moore's Revision of "Poetry" from
Twenty-nine Lines to Three*

Shocking—like an amputee.
One mustn't stare. It's a three-line
stumper.

Somebody slip a coaster
under this bar stool, I am off-
kilter!

How does my garden grow? In
the tricornered shadow of her
black hat.

Well, "omissions are not ac-
cidents," she claimed, but I do miss
the toads.

4. *Why We Don't Want Our Children to Be Poets*

Think about Stephen Dunn
washing his clean laundry at the laundromat
because he wants to write a poem
about the laundromat.

Think about yourself
thinking about Stephen Dunn.

5. Form and Theory
It's satisfying
at Wrigley Field
when the umpire
whips the brush from his pocket
and flicks red dirt
off home-shaped
home plate—
does this make me
a domestic poet?

6. Rhymes from a List Found in Odgen Nash's Papers After He Died

Who else can rhyme ennui—
can we?
Who else pairs Methuselah
with lollapalooza,
Icarus
with licorice?
Truth is, none of us.
Nash, RIP

7. On Reading Bishop's "The Fish"

Influence ends somewhere; forgive me.
For you, Miss Bishop, benediction of rainbow—
twenty-three years since your death, and it echoes—
for me, your greedy, showboat mentee,
if I hooks fishes,
delicious.

WHY WE SHOULDN'T WRITE LOVE POEMS, OR IF WE MUST, WHY WE SHOULDN'T PUBLISH THEM

How silly Robert Lowell seems in *Norton's*,
all his love vows on facing pages: his second wife,
who simmered like a wasp, his third,
the dolphin who saved him, even "Skunk Hour"
for Miss Bishop (he proposed though she was gay),
and so on, a ten-page manic zoo of love,
he should have praised less and bought a dog.

We fall in love, we fumble for a pen,
we send our poems out like Jehovah's Witnesses—
in time they return home, and when they do
they find the locks changed, FOR SALE stabbed in the yard.
Oh, aren't the poems stupid and devout,
trying each key in their pockets in plain view
of the neighbors, some of whom openly gloat.

We should write about what we know
won't change, volleyball, Styrofoam, or mildew.
If I want to write about our picnic in Alabama,
I should discuss the red-clay earth or fire ants,
not what happened while we sat cross-legged there
leaning over your surprise for me, crawfish you'd boiled with—
surprise again—three times too much crab boil—

Oh, how we thumbed apart the perforated joints
and scooped the white flesh from the red parings,
blowing on our wet hands between bites
because they burned like stars. Afterward,
in the public park, in hot sun, on red clay, inside my funnel
of thighs and skirt, your spicy, burning fingers shucked
the shell of my panties, then found my sweet meat
and strummed it, until it too was burning, burning, burning—

Ah, poem, I am weak from love, and you,
you are sneaky. Do not return home to shame me.

. . . .

III

. . . .

ON COLLABORATION: DOWNWARD DOG, HAPPY BABY, COBRA

Faulkner planted cedars along his front walk
to keep malaria-rich mosquitoes from his estate.
But here in Mississippi in fetid July, nothing's kept out
that wants in. It's dawn. I'm here because I want in

to my body, because I want to learn yoga
from you, because you want to teach it. I'm here,
though it's muggy, though we look funny
(if only to Faulkner's bourbon-besotted ghost),
though chiggers have eaten into my ankles.
Now I've lacquered them with nail polish
to suffocate the bugs, as you taught me.
A strange cure. As is yoga—which I'd ridiculed.
Now I never skip class, even when I wake woolly
from the previous night's wine.

After, I walk home, gather and inhale
from my husband's arms the warm-bread body
of our newly risen baby, lines of sleep
still mapping out her face, and I wonder—
is it the bug spray, or the deep breathing,
or this strange, fast friendship that leaves me
dazed and flushed and spry-limbed as a cat?

Is it yoga, or is it you, your frugality and red bra straps,
home-ground polenta, toe rings, and Goddess pose,
your expert read of my drafts or Downward Dog,
your raptures for the pulpy kelp off Point Reyes, California,
your ex-hippie glamour—you'd laugh, but it seems like glamour
to one who came of age in argyled Reaganomics—

No, I say, when asked if I've ever written collaboratively,

but then what have we been doing, all this heatwrung summer,
stretching on dry grass, *See where your boundaries are,*
you say, *then work past them,* stretching on dry
pages, our poems throwing sparks, kindling each other's—
the three modest letters of your name root in my lines,
lines that make you say, not entirely happily,
Sometimes I think we're the same person.

I'm moving to this town, you're moving to Sweden,
now you lead me into Dancer pose but break from it to giggle
because in my concentration I'm sticking out my tongue—
now you're in my kitchen in your sexy Chinese skirt
scissoring your fingers to show where to snip pothos
because cuttings start new plants,
another thing I never knew—

meanwhile in a California coma, your mother
has shed language like a bathrobe, perfecting Corpse pose—
They feed and wash her, you say, rubbing your sore hip,
looking for the first time anywhere near your age,
and the body can last a long time when it does no work.

Another time you confess, *I fear she'll never die.*

And here in Mississippi we feed and wash
my daughter, whose body is all work, breathing hard
as any yogi to wrest the lid from Tupperware,
biting her banana and meditating, *Ohmmmm*
(I'd always wondered where that came from),
wading into language, tossing a cracker
from her high chair tray, leaning over to spy it,
and announcing, *Uh-oh*—then, because she can,
because it feels so good to be so right,
tossing another cracker and saying *Uh-oh* again.

And farther off than California, in a land
without borders or colors on a map,
the child who died in me
and the child who died in you—

those two who wait forever in our margins—
have perhaps met across the white space
of our poems laid flush, the verso and the recto
have perhaps touched so inside the Book of Years
they find themselves less lonesome than before,
as I think we are.

If *consanguinity* means *to share blood*,
Ann, come share blood with me
in mosquito-thick Mississippi
while there's still time left
though our husbands have been looking at us strangely.

To stretch out the morning, we go to the farmer's market,
split a bushel of peaches, then eat buckwheat pancakes
at the old filling station—when the waitress mistakes me
for your daughter, I don't correct her, nor do you,
though it's true I feel guilty when my mother phones—

Next class you say, *Relax into the pose.*

So you teach me to snip plants and poems, to grasp
my insteps and roll on my back in Happy Baby pose,
while my own happy baby masters Sucking-on-Big-Toes,
then Throwing-Fit-Because-Mom-Takes-Fly-Swatter,
while I master Quiet-Sex-with-Husband-While-Baby-Watches-
    Barney,
while you master Yearning-for-Five-Babies-Grown-and-Gone,
Boxing-Up-My-Mother's-Stuff,
Dividing-with-My-Sister-these-Parcels-of-Remorse.

To return to the question, is it collaboration

if we align our soles and pull each other's wrists
to teeter-totter, give-and-take, deepen our stretch,
if we both go home and then, without discussing it,
write about birth? Is it collaboration

if later I read *collaborate* means *to labor together*?

If your next poem recalls your daughter, who is my age now,
as a newborn bunched on your chest in the bathtub,
her feet grazing your hipbones,
how you wrung the washcloth
and smoothed it on her tiny back to warm her

and if I read your poem
and envy both the image
and the daughter's bunching on your chest—

is it then collaboration, is it

if the next dawn in Cobra
I cant my hips wrongly
which brings you beside my mat
to lay your warm, ringed fingers on my back?

If *plagiarism* comes from the verb *to kidnap,*
Ann—while there's time—come
plagiarize me a little.

TELLING THE GOSPEL TRUTH

I.

Who placed this here, Bible
I nudge aside to reach the button
that brings the nurse who steadies me
on wobbly legs as I shuffle to the toilet,
grasp the handrails, and shit
for the first time since giving birth
(*You're doing fine, I know it hurts*)
while my ripped skin burns,
while my stitches strain to keep
my insides in? The nurses glide on soft shoes
and circle fingers deep on my slack belly,
pressing out the jellied black blood clots
so my uterus can shrink back.

So many women have clenched
this mattress, clamping breath
through the riptides of afterbirth.
So many women have rolled
in the half-lit predawn beneath the nurses' hands
so the blood-rich bedding
could be removed. So many women,
turning to this book.

II.

Secular is an ugly word, but there are secular things
that are not. Did I mention
the hands of the nurses on my shoulder
rolling me onto my side,
rolling me like a sea otter in a salty swell?
They called me *Honey*. They called me *Love*.
I could have been anyone to them.

III.

I want to womanize
the Bible, rend it, render it homey,
homemade, I lust to cut-and-paste.

I start with Mary, because I need her,
because I, too, am mostly mother now, appendaged
by my twenty-pound daughter
who's intent as any dentist on fingering my incisors,

or pinching my shoulder's beauty mark
that she hopes is a raisin—

I start with Mary, because she needs it,
because her role's so flat she could never get
Best Actress, which is why I delighted,
jogging past a Catholic church (as close
as I come, now), to see a statue's back
              and realize it was Mary in labor,
                              I didn't know until then
I'd been looking for Mary
                like that,
                  her robes   spread,
                  her knees by her ears,
          her veins rivering
                  the cracked and leaking
        bowl of her belly that can hold   no more,
                and the baby crowning,   skulling
through that fringe—

but reaching the statue's front I found
just another passive pietá.
No ugly agony cornering her face.

Jesus draped across her lap,
a monstrous baby, that.

IV.

Let us start with the stable.
Let it be a real stable, and let Mary be angry
at the filth of it, at dust sifting from the rafters.
Let her grow resigned as cracks of light are grouted by night,
let her grow out of mind
as the invisible fist grabs guts
and twists,
then twists harder,
let her grow scared. Let her try to remember
wading in the sea with her girlfriends, the coarse hem of her
    skirt in her hands,
the algae fingering her ankles.
Let her try, but let her fail. Let the fist
drag her under, under and under and under,
let her breath tear ragged as hot bread.

Let sweat ride the dark hairs above her lip.

Are you picturing her naked? Let her be naked.

Let us write in the animals, but not kneeling, and if they roll
their great eyes skyward

let it not be like saints in paintings

but like bored executives rising in elevators.

Yes, let the animals itch,

let them switch their tails,

let the puckered stars of their assholes flex and soft wads of shit
fall to the hay.

Let Mary's purse of stomach wrench itself inside out,

let the donkey sniff her vomit, bare yellow teeth, and turn away.

Let there be flies,

flies in the mucousy eyes of the cows,

flies skimming her slick of blood, its tributaries

with rafts of dirty hay.

Let Joseph work in his hand to feel the slick rind of the child's
skull,

then wipe his bloody fingers on her thigh.

Let her squeeze his other hand harder than she needs to.

Let her wonder who is screaming,

let her wonder if she's dying,

let her take the name

of her own sweet son
in vain.

V.

Led back to that black book, those dark waters,
why do I lean over, determined
to spy my own face, amazed,
pointing up at my own face, amazed?

O you vain girl. Bad fish.

Be brute, Lord, pierce my kisser,
reel me in. Reel me, rail me,
nail me to a tree, peel back my skin.
Oh, I am ribbed and girded, guarded—
let out my seams, gut me, Lord,
come in me to the hilt, up to the brim.

Make me like my mother-in-law
frying bacon and answering the phone,
reaching for her pen and Thomas Kinkade lighthouse pad
to add to the prayer chain—
Sally's mom,
cancer real bad in stom. now, end near.
Then, returning to the stove, her lips moving,
stirring out lumps for her husband's grits.

Make me like her, bowl scraped of ego,
stirring, stirring, stirring,
stirring her smoothness in,
then brushing the hair back from my forehead—
lovely bafflement who makes faith seem easy
the way thin people seem naturally thin.

VI.

I'm tired of the hip cynicism
of atheists, tired of metafiction,

of winks at the camera,
of poems using dinner knives
to check for spinach in their teeth.

I want to reclaim the optimism
of the grand old religions, I want exclamations,
exultations, belly laughs, shaking fists,
tears for all my friends, tears on the house!

The next time a student asks
how to become a writer, I will say,
    Sit in a white room
          without paper
        and think of the poacher
              who shot the wing off the bald eagle.
            Who must have seen
                      he wrecked his trophy
       and, disgusted,
     did not offer it
              a second bullet
           but thrashed off deeper into the forest
wearing his expensive
        forest–colored clothes.

Then   think of the man from the wild bird sanctuary
                           who found the eagle,
                  sutured its ragged wingstub,
                      fed the awkward hopping thing
      for years.
                And, before it died, harnessed it
                  in a hang glider and took it to the mountain
so one last time
          its hollow bones could float,
so one last time
its eyes could scour the forest floor from hunter's height,
so one last time
            its talons could tear the gauzy cloak of sky,
                    flying in the face
                              of God,
that one last time.

              Think of the poacher, think of the birder.
     Alternate,
shortening the intervals.
Don't forget to breathe.

When you can hold both of these men
in the palm of your mind

at the same time,

Love,

come find me,

and teach me.

VII.

I miss the altar boys swinging the censers like Jacob Marley's
   ghost rattling his chains,
I miss the misselletes in their leatherette covers, and the church
   bulletin with ads from Catholic businesses,
I miss my family maneuvering into a pew on the center aisle
   then acting surprised when chosen to bring communion to
   the altar,
I miss the communion host and its host-house, the monstrance,
I miss the word *monstrance,*
I miss the deacon flanking the priest and bowing the wine
   chalice to our bowing heads, then rotating it in his
   handkerchief, a half-concession to germs,
all while the long fashion show of communion pauses, steps,

pauses, steps,
I miss most of all the singing
and the comfortable boredom in the frusty stained air with the
    occasional wren darting between the archivolts
and I miss the altar boys swinging the censers
like Jacob Marley's ghost rattling his chains

VIII.

If we can fill in Mary and cross out Abraham
(Abraham—the one rewarded
        because he'd kill his child to please his God;
Me—one who split her body open
        to please the tiny God who wanted out)—

if the Bible's a draft,
a mirror, a fortune cookie, a wishing well, an optical illusion
                where I see crows fleeing,
where you see doves returning—

does it lose its power?

Is it possible to mend a cloth so often
                              nothing's left but the mending?

At Notre Dame, our fight song ended,
"While her loyal sons are marching onward to victory"
and I was one of those who yelled, "and daughters"—

so likewise I decided
        to stop picturing God as a white-haired old white man
        stop singing *Him* in hymns
picture instead a genderless breeze who valued
women and animals and gays and birth control and masturbation,

I didn't know then that the threads I pulled
                        ten years later would still be unraveling—

IX.

One spring a pair of bluebirds came
to the birdhouse on the fence,
and built their nest just like I'd hoped they would.
And, just like I'd hoped, lined it
with grasses and pine straw
and hair that I pulled from my brush,
and then the five globes of their soon-to-be,
shells blue and wishful as airmail envelopes,
shells lightly freckled. For fourteen days,
such expectancy, the mother warmed them
with her body, and when she hunted
or chased off the bully mockingbird,
I'd survey the silver-dollar hole
for pecking translucent beaks
and frizzy heads wearing shell helmets
like bluebirds in cartoons.

Then one day, the mother's shrieking,
in and out of the birdhouse, her panicked feints and darts—
I looked and found the eggs,
crushed. Lord

knows why. A snake
would have swallowed them,
not left the nest
brimming with that terrible yolky stew. . . .

That spring I, too, lost my soon-to-be,
my blood on that New Orleans bed
bright as Mardi Gras,
my blood pulpy and strung out as the beads
my leaping husband caught for me at the Muses parade,
the beads most coveted with the dangling plastic baby charm,
the beads that I wore chevroned
between my newly tender breasts
as we hand-held down Pirate's Alley,
the charm, when we strolled, tapping
the stomach-of-our-secret, the locus-of-our-hope—

but back at the Hotel Monteleone
how I cramped and keened, fetally, fatally,
how I battered the mattress in my sorrow and my rage,
while my husband paged the midwife,
while the maids knocked to make up our room—

and whom could I supplicate, whom could I implore,
whom could I bargain with in my bloody terror,
whom could I blame, screaming bloody murder,
whom could I curse for stealing my firstborn—

and the midwife phoned to say,
Bring the clots in a cup to a hospital
to see if all fetal matter
was expelled
or if you'll need a D & C. . . .

Yes, yes, a D & C.
Then came the mulling months,
the moon rolling across the sky
like a gaudy egg.

Spring, it came late that year.
In wiped-out Illinois, it snowed, it snowed,
it snowed some more. Such heavy snow,
our carport groaned beneath it,
then fell hard to its knees.
I waited
for slush, for thaw, for forsythia

to knot like a whip or a rosary, I waited
soberly, desperately,
and—because it had to—

spring did return.
And so did the bluebirds,

and something fluttered in me
to see them gather pine straw and start to build,
fastidious as tailors with pins in their mouths.
Soon, five new eggs
gemmed the new nest—a parable—
hope is a thing with feathers—

except
several days later, it happened again—the eggs
all gored, all galled.

Then it was winter again, and I knew
the next spring I wouldn't see
the wizened bluebirds. . . .

but I was wrong. They returned. They keep returning.
Is it stupidity, is it instinct, is it faith?
Five nests, now, and twenty-five dead nestlings.

I want to tell that mother *Do not build here anymore.*
I want to tell her, *Please, I can't do it one more time.*
Twice now I've dreamt that I flew to her and told her
It's okay to move if your home's gone bad.

X.

And now—here she is—
  Miss Claire of the Sticky Digits,
  Genius of the Light Switch,
  Victor of the Safety Latch—
and she's pooching her lips to say, emphatically, *ball,*
and using her whole arm to point, emphatically, to her ball,
and also to cantaloupes and doorknobs and casters,
  ball ball ball—
   each vista gifted with naming, grafted with meaning—

and now I foresee
rolling toward me
that ball of questions
I duck, I flinch,
that ball of questions
I just can't catch

                                Dying? I don't
think about it,
                       I go shopping for shoes.

Ann, smart friend, read a poem I wrote about religion,
knew it was simple and wrong—

What it would take,
        what it would really take, to engage with this subject . . .

Because I'm still not ready.
I'm playing alongside my baby.
I'm wearing shoes so new they bear
a price tag shaped like a coffin.
They are walking shoes, I suppose,
but I haven't gotten very far.
Whither shall I go?

Whither shall I go?

(*Come to Mommy, Claire*).

Whither.
                    Whither.

RIDDLE, TWO YEARS LATER

"I am a riddle in nine syllables"

—SYLVIA PLATH, *"Metaphors"*

O, it was a riddle, but I lost

               syllable count.

        That calendar was thrown away.

I went to have a picture made

           of echoes, expecting

                 a pearl necklace!

                 a happy dinghy, tethered!

          But the rope

snapped, crossed

   to the other side. Unmoored,

              this riddle.

                I was a garden

        blighted in April,

             a poisoned well.

    I came back from vacation to a burgled house.

No, worse than burgled.

             What's the word in English

                for *worse than burgled*?

The technician's cursor flitted across the screen.

I was an empty stage, curtain drawn back,

              X

        of fluorescent tape to show

       where the star should have stood. But the star

didn't show.

The show,

        no,

    it didn't go on.

I was all about blocking. Bad blocking.

              Houselights, please.

At the end of this riddle

      there was no punch line.

         Or there was a sucker-punch line.

Rising from the toilet

the day after the riddle

        was sliced and sucked out,

(the doctor used the French name

        but the French, it didn't help)

    a piece of this riddle,

        elephantine, rubbery, fell

    on the toe of my pump.

          And there were three months

          before I could even *try*

            to make a new riddle.

One out of five women will get this riddle,

and they are the sorry ones.

      The echo made from a picture

        made of an echo: o   o   o

THE GODS WATCH US
THROUGH THE WINDOW

We sit at the table with the fourth side open,
the perfect family show. Claire belts "Twinkle, Twinkle,"
How I wa wa (mumble) *are!*
We beam like stars. Isn't she gifted? Isn't life great?

What a large target we make.
The great dramas all begin like this:
a surfeit of happiness, a glass-smooth pond
just begging for a stone.

MAKING AN EGG FOR CLAIRE, SUNNY-SIDE UP

I find a blood smear on the monstrous yolk.

Dead child, first love, there's a place for you, too,
at my table, but how shall I call you?
You died without ears
in a town so far away and cold with snow.

THE PRESENTATION

You were eighteen in a California
of Christian Science mothers and eucalyptus trees,
it was the annunciation, the 60s descended in feathers
where you lay in a California it would never be again
after you got up and that green-hungry boy
brushed the rich dirt from your shoulders, chest, and blondness—
a moment others—say, your mother—might call "seedy,"
as *fuck* comes from Old English, *to plant seeds.*

Within hours, within you,
the cell, smaller than a decimal point,
began its long division.
But you know how unforgiving
math can be. Just one small mistake
and it won't add up.

Isn't there a poem by Hass
where he writes of long division
and carrying the remainder? I bet you've read it, Ann.
I bet you carried the remainder
knowing it meant forever,
carried it through California, Virginia, Mississippi, now Sweden—
carried it alongside each of your later babies

who learned to make room for their spirit-sibling,
learned that though you suckled it
your other breast had milk enough for them.

0   0   0   0   0   0   0   0

Smaller than a decimal.
Your Jennifer Lisa, had she lived,
would be old enough to have a child
who would be old enough to babysit my first child,
had it lived.

It's about math, solving for the unknown, for X,
and, for me, for XX or XY—

your baby had a gender and a name.

0   0   0   0   0   0   0   0

Maybe there were no eucalyptus trees.
I'm imagining things again. Maybe it was on your bed,

the movie theatre's duct-taped seats, the hood of his MG—
but I'd bless that child's conception with the dignity of green.

Once the summer after college you were traveling in Spain,
all the hotels too full, too costly,
and so like any other good tanned tired resourceful pilgrim
you crawled under a fruit stand
and slept like a baby with your backpack for a pillow—
dreaming of the party on the Barcelona rooftop,
dreaming of the man there who fed you aioli
(he poured a stream of olive oil into the egg yolk while whisking,
added a touch more pale green oil, kept whisking,
his flexible brown wrist,
the moment glistening, growing thick).
It rained toward morning and you woke under the wooden stand
with the pomegranate's clear jelly
smeared across your hip bones and your thighs—
no, no, wait, that was me. That self-same seedy girl.

Another night in California
a man promised you something marvelous,
so he carried you in his red truck
far along the desert road, parked on the shoulder,

led you to barbed wire, lifted the top strand,
and set his boot on the lower, so yes you bent, stepped through
that grinning mouth, and found the something marvelous,
the hot springs, bubbling, steaming, spitting primordial,
you lowered your body into that scalding champagne,
leaned your head back on the hard earth
with light-headed stars that rushed you, popping and humming,
and not until the cattle circled you
with their deep-welled, lugubrious eyes
did you realize you were naked, and desire
to go back home.

        No, that too was me, all me.
I'm not sure what I'm saying anymore,
not sure why I'm lying,
why this fits, or doesn't fit.
I guess just this—you were eighteen under the eucalyptus,
I was twenty-eight and married,
but our equations
could have been inversed, and other inputs
would have yielded different outputs
from our bodies:

a theory of probability
which strikes through my theory of punishment,
which keeps me wondering—

When numbers don't add up,
how far back in the ledger must we go
to find the cause?
What highway stop?

0   0   0   0   0   0   0   0

If only we could look it up.
If you brought it to Sweden,
open your *Handbook for Writers*
to any page you like—

15b: How Can I Proofread for Little Words I Omit
     Unintentionally?

15d: How Can I Avoid Shifts in Tense and Mood?

15j: How Can I Avoid Shifts in Person and Number?

0   0   0   0   0   0   0   0

All this obsessive navel gazing—
a few months back I vowed:
No More Poems About Claire.
And now I write and write about this "it."
I do not think that's what I meant.
I'm getting it all wrong again.

If "it" had lived, of course, there'd be no Claire.
It's all about the math.
And when I think how desperately
she fought that day, she fought to stay—
Tommy out of town and Claire put down
for a good long nap and I was glad,
glad to get my work done, a good long nap, Claire put down,
   and I was glad,
then perhaps the nap too long, not quite so good, not quite so
   glad,
I checked on her
all wrong how
now I couldn't wake her
her temperature 105 that can't be right

soon shivering, slivering, her eyes gone bad,
blue, slick, slim death
shaking hollow her her raspy breath like something tearing
please talk wake up
I will not let you join the other
I filled the sink with ice *Where is the fucking ambulance*
I held her down and down
until her fever broke
us both so
helped me
God.

0   0   0   0   0   0   0   0

The sound of that ice cracking in her bath.
Is the sound of my life, cracking.

Understand: I wouldn't trade her for the ghostchild.
But I, revisionist, recidivist, cannot help but solve for X—

and feel disloyal to Claire,
and guilty when others suffer much later miscarriages

yet recover better,
without needing all this noise—

Oh, I've botched grief's ratio. My failure
of proportion surprising, shaming me.

0   0   0   0   0   0   0   0

1. *How many children do you have?*
There's just one answer, and it's wrong.

2. *How many children do you have?*
Ann, I'm sending you this grid
of imaginary numbers,
whole notes.

3. *How many children do you have?*
We'll make a place where they can count.

4. *How many children do you have?*
Zero's always where you start
and though you never say it,

it's always there. The zero's there.
Zero at the bone. The zero counts.

5. *How many children do you have?*
I came across my school notes
on *The Waste Land,* with
"the excised Fresca section,
the felt absence at the center
of the poem." And beside that,
I'd doodled a rococo question mark—
not yet understanding
how absence can define itself,
how, the more you put
behind, beside, in front of it
the more pronounced its corners grow,
the edges sharper honed.
Touch them and you'll bleed.

6. *How many children do you have?*
The belly of the hole puncher
packed with paper circles,
byproducts, remainders, felt
felt absences.

0   0   0   0   0   0   0   0

If the dead baby is far enough along, they make you look at it.
My friend David said that in his wife's hospital room
they returned with the child wrapped in swaddling clothes,
wearing her pink cotton cap.
They held her up in bright halo light, then slowly
unwrapped her, turning her to show
the knuckles of her open spine.
Then with ginger fingers they rolled the cap's thin brim
to display the soft ripe plum of head
where the pit of skull peeked through.

This is what they call *the presentation.*
It's supposed to help.

Me, I wasn't quite so far along.
The blanket of anesthesia
was tucked under my chin.
They sliced my baby, sucked it with a hose.

So now I carry rosemary for remembrance,
daisy for innocence,

ivy for fidelity,
marigold for grief,
so now I need to know—
where shall I lay me down
my bright bouquet?

I half-recall the squat round bin
beneath the stirruped cot.
The kind of bin you open with your foot.

0   0   0   0   0   0   0   0

When the baby died in me, I couldn't talk about it,
begged Tommy, *Don't talk about it*—
so why now? Why now write about this "it"?

Perhaps because whole months have passed
since Claire's baptism in cracking ice,
since nights of holding the hand mirror

beneath the sleeping beauty's nose,
which must mean I've gained faith in real live breath—
She likes it here, she fought to stay—

Perhaps because I thought I should put the death behind me
until meeting you, Ann, and talking about Jennifer Lisa,
dead these thirty-seven years, and now I know it will always be
   before me—

and I feel like the girl who raised her hand in school
and, by the time she was called on, forgot what she wanted to say,
but due to the teacher's prodding, came up with something
   better—

so now I've talked so much I'm tired. All my life
I've stared at this white page, yet I swear
I'd never noticed how very like a headstone it could be.

And all this time I've solved for X
which stands for the unknown—
but it also stands for *kiss*.

I think at last that I could rest.
Now, I'll lay me down
my bright bouquet.

IV

HAVING WORDS WITH CLAIRE

Magnificent new word I trace into pollen on the car hood
because all is spring and budding through the beds
of your gums are two new teeth

word-of-the-day which, after reading my lips, you mimic
and I mimic your mimicry, becoming your child

word that grows siblings,
they tumble in your wet mouth
like wash in the Razorback Laundromat where I used to go
    with your father
before he was your father
when we were grad-school-poor
and where a man who *liked the way my delicates looked,*
who wanted to *share a load,*
one day filched my panties—
so your father and I opened a Sears card
and maxed it out buying our own machine
that for six years now has washed our skivvies
and for nearly a year has washed your T-shirts small as washcloths,
your socks like finger puppets

word I can't make out
that you shout while banging your bottle on the baby gate,
reminding me of the Julia B. Tutwiler Women's Prison
and the words I learned there while teaching poetry
after being frisked by guards down to my naked toes on the
    concrete:
all in my grill (to be in a person's space)
flip da script (to lose one's temper)
true dat (expression of agreement)
bling bling (something expensive, classy, luxurious)
bout-it bout-it (to understand)

words I will bout-it bout-it
words you will pen (your still-to-be-revealed handwriting),
carve into the spritzy night air with sparklers, toe in the sand,
words you will ride, a naked horse in naked rain,
words you will rest in, a hammock waffling your thighs,
words you will home in, and where you can bury, I hope,
the shrapnel of the word-grenades I will hurl at you, forgive me

words learned from The Wiggles
the Australian kiddie band that does the most rocking rendition
of "Heads, Shoulders, Knees and Toes"

words that have licked my wrists like a puppy and will lick yours
words that are spells for grade school enemies so their teeth
   drop out
words you'll misspell
boasts and dares and unladylike words, I wish them on you

crosswords, cross words, words of dead poets, words for dead pets,
words to a mirror, a pillow, to the shoulder seam
of a dancing partner smelling of mown grass and Old Spice

your favorite word, who knows why,
once I asked my ESL students their favorite English word
and the Colombian woman who trembled like a petal
shouted, surprising us all, *Handkerchief!*

the splendid word of her name, *Floralba*

all the splendid words in all the locked rooms of languages,
Diminutive Pugilist, knock down those doors

words for birds and their Latin names, too,
does *vase* rhyme with *gauze* or *case*,
you must choose

wrong words—
I always thought to get a good price you "chew it down,"
picturing a pie, not a slur on Jews

words that count or count you out,
words that turn on you or turn you on,
words that will make your juices prink and breed
slooshy between the clasped red purse of your deepskinfold

words others will use to name this part and, by naming, colonize,
words you can reject, or reclaim like Dr. Evermore
who makes art from sewer caps and bicycle chains,
or like Linda in Galesburg who sent the coolest baby gift, red
    cowboy hat size XXXS,
and who says with words and without, *I'm a dyke*

poisonous words, like the n-word,
which your father, young and terrified at his first teaching job,
five classes at an all-black college,
would, when he finally slumped into exhausted sleep,
script onto the blackboard of his nightmare

words that will teach you to crave the absence of words,
words like waves, like sand, like spume, like salt
in wounds, on rims with limes,
with crumpets trumpets O strumpet spring

words that make nothing happen

others that make too much,
churning that pre-speech underworld
where once we floated like deep sea divers
holding hands in that original buddy system,
eyeballing marvels vague and desirable,
all was gesture and guessture
and I was necessary as oxygen, I alone could translate,
my mothertongue quick to claim as a cat's

words you tie in nets that airlift us gasping
into the blinking Helen Keller sun
where anything that can be held can be spelled
with the fluorescent alphabet magnets on the fridge

and where I learn to share you
with listening audiences everywhere
both because it is the fulfillment of my life
and because I have no voice in this matter.

SAY CHEESE

I've documented everything—each tooth,
your first haircut, your first bath in the sink.
Later when you claim neglect, I've proof
of my side for your husband or your shrink.

DRIVING THE SPOON INTO HER MOUTH

I find my own garage door
has been open for a while.

FIRST DAY AT DAYCARE

My daughter comes home smelling like
another woman's perfume.

LO, THE CHILD DISPLAYETH CUNNING, PARADISE IS FAYLING

Got her, trapped between my knees
after chasing her down the long hallway
where she's scampered with my lipstick,

when did she learn this snatch and ditch,
this mature desire, just last month she clamored
for nothing more salacious than ice cream

or another book before Night Night—
now she shakes me off—*You little brat*—
I'm prying each small claw from the silver tube

but she wasn't born yesterday and to prove it
head-butts my jaw, then kicks my kneecap,
Ah now I see it, the family resemblance

in her flushed and defiant profile, the same one
I marched past my mother in sixth grade
after eighth grader Jimmy Greenwood

lured me into the boathouse
on our school field trip, the oar of his tongue
scooping out the hull of my cheeks,

his hand sliding portside into my jean pocket
where yes I'd stashed my mother's stolen lipstick,
and my hand skating like a water spider

over the harsh and straining denim
of his fly, sizing up that other tube,
tube most forbidden so most ardently desired—

what power I took on with that knowledge
before the indifferent bus dropped me
at the end of our long driveway,

at least it seemed long to me then
when at the other end
the mother was waiting waiting to come out.

DADDY PHASE,

we say,
as the child slaps the bottle from my hand
but opens wide for Daddy,

Daddy Phase,
perfectly natural, just a stage,
as she calls for him upon waking,
Daddy Phase as he rises to her, tired but flattered,
pretending I'm the lucky one, inviting me to keep sleeping

as if I care to keep sleeping
on the stale white bread
of this marriage bed, *Daddy Phase*—

me, I'm a huge bland lawn jockey
and she, she is a perfect
size zero, gigging the tireless horse of her father
back and forth across the kitchen tile

I think she just pretends to be a baby

I would like to pitch a fit
when she ducks my kiss

my lips two fat hot dogs
cooling at the drive-thru,

but would *she* bother to notice?
Would she feel *compelled* to empathize?
No,
because she's a BABY,
it's a brilliant plan

A determined competitor, I
diversify my offerings

Have you seen this one? I ask her,

apparently she has

If only she still drank my milk
still drank my bloodwarm milk
then I could squeeze her, squeeze her, squeeze her

Oh, there were entire years before she existed,
years of the single fare, years of the road trip,
years of the fishnets and the fake ID,

the Doc Martens, the come-as-you-are,
the backpack, hipflask, do-not-disturb,

I used to be a restaurant hostess Oh I had the power then,
tapping a pencil on my bottom lip
or slipping it whisperingly down the waiting list,
the tips that I palmed,
the gents that I stacked like quarters on a pool table—
one crook of my long red nail,
how they would leap to my side

but now,
now we're in the *Daddy Phase*

so now I remember
that each spring I'd discover
in the restaurant coat check room
some sad brown parka,
forgotten, forsaken—

so now I feel the elbows
of the empty wire hangers,
so now I hear them titter and hiss

THE GODS TELL ME,
YOU WILL FORGET ALL THIS

You lie, I answer. I remember circling the Q-tip dipped in alcohol around the stump of her umbilical cord. I remember the newborn diapers with the half-moon cut out so as not to chafe that black knot. Those hips the breadth of my hand. I remember the terror of trimming her nails.

No, they say, you are forgetting. Already you have lost the trip to Indiana, when she was five weeks old. Tommy drove, you sat in the back leaning over her car seat because you needed to look at her as she slept or you would disappear—

Sometimes even now I sit in the backseat with her—

It's different now. You sat in the backseat with her and you were sucking on a Tootsie Pop—

Yes it was a cherry Tootsie Pop

and although you knew it was wrong you touched it to her tiny mouth

I remember her tiny mouth

and she who had never tasted anything but breast milk

My breast milk

got the scent of that sweetness and her blind blunt tongue emerged and bumped against it, withdrew, bumped against it, withdrew.

Yes, that's how it was.

And you were fascinated at your own bad hand, holding the red ball there to her red tongue.

Yes, I was fascinated. Tommy heard my guilty giggle and looked in the rearview, so I lowered my hand. Later, we pulled over at a rest stop and I sat on a picnic table and suckled her, the yellow waffle-weave blanket over my shoulder, her tiny tummy warm against my own warm flesh. Afterward, I hesitated, but showed him the Tootsie Pop. He hesitated, then took it, held it to her lips and we giggled together. For months to come, when she was asleep and we missed her and it was all we could do to keep from waking her, he would imitate the tentacle-tongue slipping between the lips, not pointed with intent but flat, world-free, allowing the pleasure to meet it. Then retracting. Then emerging again. Ah, it was sweet, because she was so very small, and because it was our secret, our original sin, Claire's first solid food.

It was sweet because you understood you could hurt her and that made her more yours. And just yesterday you realized you hadn't mentioned that for several weeks so you said, "Do the tongue," but his imitation was off somehow. Though you both tried, neither of you could quite correct it. And so it is gone forever.

That's not true, I say. We'll recapture the tongue. Besides, I'm writing everything down.

That old lie. You'll look at the words and they'll crawl off the page. But take solace that the pain fades, too. You can't relive childbirth.

But I *want* to relive childbirth. I want everything back, every blessed thing.

It's too much for one person.

Let me try.

You're too greedy. And it doesn't work that way. The infant is disappearing as we speak. She is more ours than yours now.

Fine, I say, not meaning it. I'll have another.